In for Winter, Out for Spring

In for Winter, Out for Spring

By ARNOLD ADOFF

Illustrations by JERRY PINKNEY

Harcourt Brace & Company

SAN DIEGO   NEW YORK   LONDON

Requests for permission to make copies of
any part of the work should be mailed to:
Permissions Department,
Harcourt Brace & Company, 6277 Sea Harbor Drive,
Orlando, Florida 32887-6777.

First Harcourt Brace paperback edition 1997

Library of Congress Cataloging-in-Publication Data
Adoff, Arnold.
In for winter, out for spring/by Arnold Adoff;
illustrations by Jerry Pinkney. — 1st ed.
p.   cm.
Summary: This collection of poems, told from the
perspective of a young girl, celebrates family life
throughout the yearly cycle of seasons.
ISBN 0-15-238637-8
ISBN 0-15-201492-6 (pbk.)
1. Seasons — Juvenile poetry. 2. Children's poetry, American.
[1. Seasons — Poetry. 2. Family life — Poetry. 3. American poetry.]
I. Pinkney, Jerry, ill. II. Title.
PS3551.D6616   1991
811'.54 — dc20   90-33185

A C E F D B

Printed in Singapore

The illustrations in this book were done in pencil, watercolor,
color pencil, and pastel on 130 lb. Arches hot-press paper.

The text type was set in Berling by Thompson Type, San Diego, California.

The display type was set in Pictor Medium by Central Graphics, San Diego, California.

Color separations were made by Bright Arts, Ltd., Singapore.

Printed and bound by Tien Wah Press, Singapore

This book was printed on Leykam recycled paper,
which contains more than 20 percent postconsumer waste and has a total
recycled content of at least 50 percent.

Production supervision by Warren Wallerstein and Pascha Gerlinger

Typography by Michael Farmer

For my mother and father: Rebecca Stein Adoff and Aaron Jacob Adoff
—A. A.

In celebration of the family
—J. P.

I Am The Youngest   So They Call
                    Me   All
                    Day Long

My Name Is Rebecca At Breakfast
                        Time
            Becky By Lunch
                    But
        Becka
        Beck
        Beck Come
            Wash   Your
                      Neck
        Is Daddy's Supper
                Song

                I Like My Real
                Name   Short
                And   My Hair
                Real   Long
I Am The Youngest   And I Belong

This House   Is The   Center

Is My   Home
Is Where
My   Toys
Belong
Is Where
My   Brother
Aaron
Sleeps

This House
Has   Food
Has   Mom
And
Dad
Has   My
Great
Bed   This   Winter
Season
Under
Snow

We   Know
This House   Is The   Center

The First Flakes   Are Falling   On Our Heads

As Daddy Stands Me Up Against The Cold Back
                                                    Door
For My Morning Measurement
                                        Of Course This
                                                Head
                                                Line
                        Is   Higher   Than The Last
                                                Head
                                                Line
But This Will Be The Last Time   Until   The
                                                Snows
Are Over   And We Can Get Outside Again   For
                                Morning   Chores

Now I Know That Daddy And Aaron   Will   Bake
Their   Best   Cookies   And Momma Will   Make
The Most Crisp   Chicken   That Helps To Grow
                                                Us   All
In   This   Long   Winter   House   Under   Snow

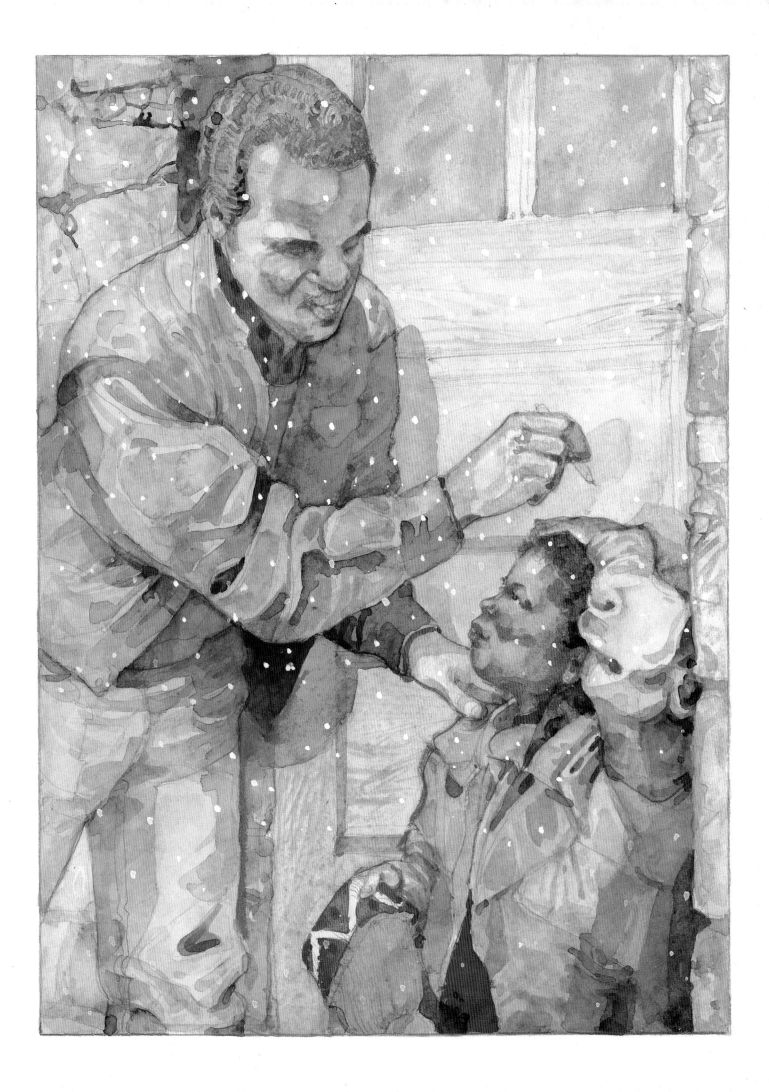

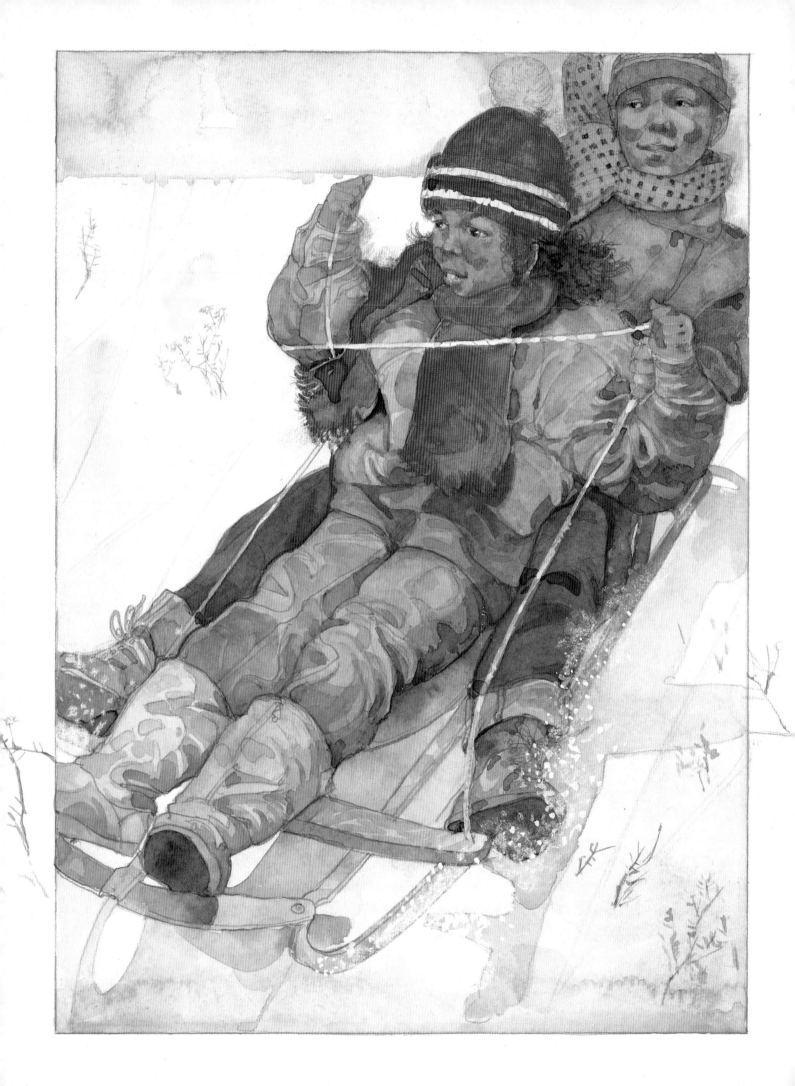

In The Ending   Of This Evening Snow

I Like My Long Hair Free   Let It Blow
                            Let It Blow

In The   Last   Light
Of The   Last   S u n
                   Glow   Let It Blow
                            Let It Blow

I Am Some Wild Horse
Running From   Fence
                      To
                Fence
My Hot Breath
       Blowing
In The Wild
       Evening
       Freeze
       And I Am Free   As My L o n g
                        Hair   Blows
       Like That Horse Mane In The
                        Snow   Breeze
                        Let It Blow
                        Let It Blow

In The Ending   Of This Evening Snow
I Like My Long Hair Free

Mouse   Under The House   Mouse   In The House

One Day   In This Coldest Winter   But In Our
                                               W a r m
                                               Kitchen

Daddy   Screamed   A Perfect
Cartoon Scream   And Dropped   The Heavy Cream
                   And Dropped   His C a k e   Pan
                                      A n d Ran
                               Out Of Our
                                     W a r m
                                     Kitchen
               Faster   Than   The   Mouse Was
               R u n n i n g   The   Other Way

Later On   We Explored Outside   And Found A Crack In The
      Foundation Stones Big Enough For A Whole Family Of Cold
And Hungry Mice   And All Their Luggage   They Must Have
Traveled Through The Heating Ducts That Lie   Under The
      House From Room To Room Until They Settled In The Warm
      Kitchen In Back Of The Cabinet Next To The W a r m Oven
Their
Nest Was Between Two Bags Of Daddy's   Best   Cake   Flour
And An Old Pot   Full   Of   Soft   White   String   I Think
                  They Were Planning To Stay Until Spring

Out   For   Spring

I
Sing And   Shout
              About
              Time
      For
      Big
      Bad   Winter
             Times
             To
             End
I
Send
This   Spring
              Song
              Out
      For
      All
      To   Shout
      And   Sing

Out   For   Spring
Out   For   Spring
Out   For   Spring

After The Last Hard Freeze   In Early Spring Weather

When The Ground Has Softened   And The Sun Is Strong
Enough To Warm The Open Field We Dig Up The   Young
                                                Sumac
                                                Saplings

From Their   Winter Places   Beside The Old
                                        Fence

And Carry Them To   New
                Places In   Our   Front
                                    Yard

I Am Digging Holes With Daddy   Spreading Roots   Out
I Am Filling   Holes With Rich Dirt And Peat
                                    Moss   Pouring
                                                In
                        Green Fertilizer Water
                        For A Healthy Start
                        In Their New Homes

I Am Digging Holes With Daddy

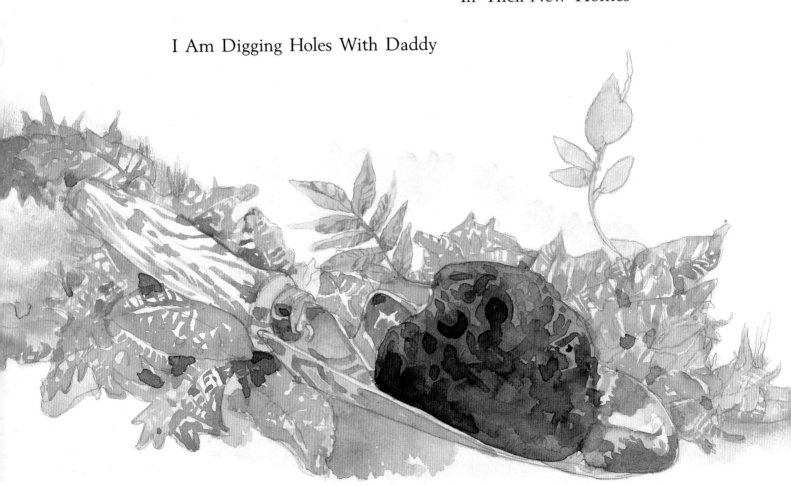

She   Was   Hungry   And   Cold

Alone
Along The Edge   Of Granny's Field
A   Tired   Puppy   Chased
By   Fresh   Farm   Dogs   And   Their
        P l o w i n g   Farmer
                            To My
                            Yard

I   Am   Building   Her   New   House
And   Will   Take   Care Of Her From
                N o w On
        And Momma Says She Can
                            Stay

                            Stray

I Hear The Usual   Thump

And Know That One   More
                      R o b i n
Has Hit The Glass   Door
In Love   With   Its   Own
                 Reflection

This Bird Seems To
                 Be
R e s t i n g
     On The
     Ground
T e s t i n g   Its Bent
                W i n g

I   Bring
A   Dish
Of Water And Watch For
             C a t s

On   May   Day

This
Monarch
Butterfly
Flew
Into Our
Open Door
And
Through
The
House To
Land On
Top
Of
My
Open
Hand

Of
Course
I S e t
It F r e e

The Morning Wind   From The West

Is Bringing The Smoke
Of The Paper Mills
              And
              The
                    Smoke
Of Burning
      Plastic And Coal

Some Days   The   Air   Is So Good
It Is The Best Cure For Bad Dreams
But This Morning
      This Air   Is
              Bad
              For All Living Things
              The
              Breeze   Brings   Ills
              The Wind   Seems   Sad
              To Be Blowing Our Way

We Stay In For The Rest Of The Day

My Brother Aaron Runs Outside To Tell Us There Is A Severe
Thunder
Storm
Warning

Just Announced On The Radio While We Were Out
U n d e r
A Perfectly Blue Sky
We Know How Fast The   Weather Can Change   How
Fast Those   Storms   Can
Blow Across These   Corn
Fields   E v e r y   Spring

We Bring   Our   Books
And Toys Inside   And
Listen To   The   Noon
News
Between   The   Soup
And   Sandwiches
And
Try   To   Only   Think
A b o u t
Our   Lunch

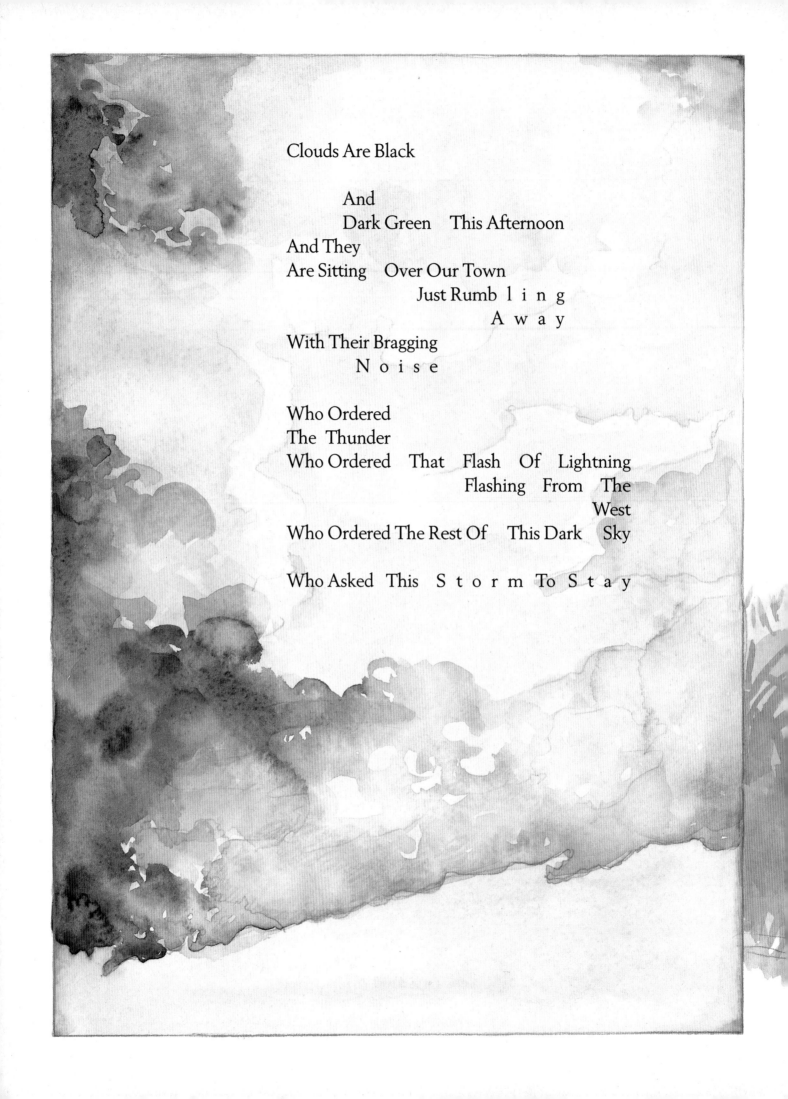

Clouds Are Black

And
Dark Green   This Afternoon
And They
Are Sitting   Over Our Town
                    Just Rumb l i n g
                            A w a y
With Their Bragging
          N o i s e

Who Ordered
The Thunder
Who Ordered That Flash Of Lightning
                    Flashing   From   The
                                    West
Who Ordered The Rest Of   This Dark   Sky

Who Asked This S t o r m To S t a y

The Bottoms   Of My Sneaks   Are   Green

Then
The Bottoms   Of My Sweat   Are   Green
                              Socks

Then
The Bottoms   Of My F e e t   Turn   Green
                                   As

When
          My Sneaks And   Socks   Come   Off
                                      Half   Way
                                      Down
                                      This
                                      Field   Of
                                      Fresh

                                                Green
                                                Grass

                                      And
                                      Dew

My Momma Mows
This   N e w
          Summer
          Morning

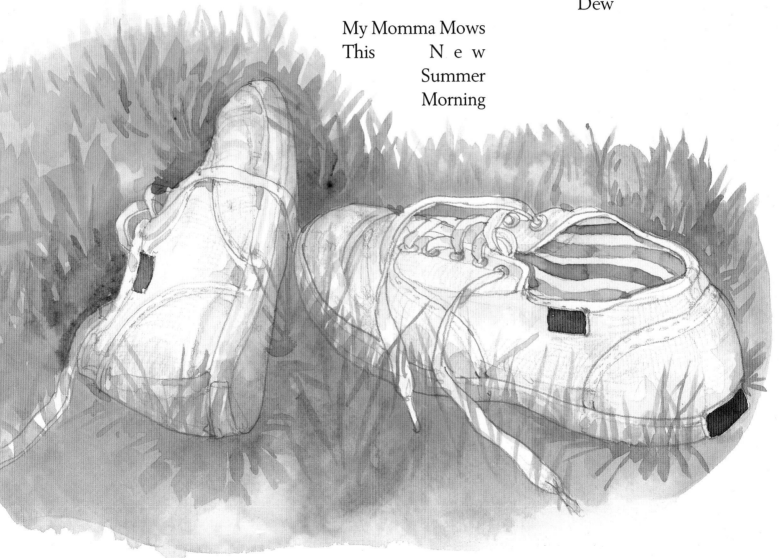

Daddy   Is Tall   Has Shoulders   Strong Hands

But I Am   The   Mulberry   Girl
Riding   On His High Shoulders   Under These
                                        Tree
                                        Treats
                                        These
                              H a n g i n g
                        B r a n c h e s
                                        These
                              H a n g i n g
                                        Eats

So   Dry   This   July

                This

                      Drought

Has   Cracked

The   Ground

Has   Killed

        Young

          Trees

When It   Finally   Does

                  Rain

Good   And   Hard

We Run   Into   The   Yard

To   Soak   Our

Dusty   Feet   In   Mud

          Up   To

            Our

            Knees

Volunteers   One

Black Raspberry Bushes   Blackberries
Wild Strawberries   Wild Onion Grass
Dandelions   Mint   Catnip   Maples
                    F o r S h a d e
Elm And Ash   And Sunflowers   Daisies
Wild Roses   Poison Ivy So Thick You
                Know To Stay Far Away
Black Walnut
            Trees

                For
                Our Cakes   And Hungry
                    S q u i r r e l s
                Who Will
                    Stay   For The Wet
                        W i n t e r

And
All The Trees   And Weeds   And   Wild
                        F l o w e r s

And Their Blowing   Seeds

Volunteers   Two

Clouds Of Flies When The Hot Dogs Are Done
And We Are Ready To Eat
Mosquitoes And Bugs That Fly In Your Ears
And Gnats
And Mayflies
And Devilflies That Bite   In
The
Heat
Of   A Dry   July
After
noon

Bees All Do Their Famous Work
And Worms Are Washed   Up
After
Rains
And Spiders
Spiders
Spiders

One Night

They Are
Out
All
Together
On
Some
Signal At
The
Same Time
Flashing
And
Flashing
And
Blinking
Bright in
This
Late
Summer
Night
Long
Past My
Bed Time
Late This
Night
Of
The
Fireflies

I Know That Summer Is The Famous Growing Season

But These Fall Days Are For The Gathering   Of
                                            The
                                            Last
                                            Of
                                            The

Grown And Ripe Tomatoes
For G r a n n y ' s Tomato
              Preserves   Corn and Beans   To Be
              Canned   In Mason Jars

I Get To Climb The Old Apple Tree   For The Best
                   Yellow   Delicious Apples
For Daddy's Pie
For Momma's Apple Honey Buns
For My C l i m b i n g F u n

Daddy Carries His Empty Basket

On His Head
And Pretends To Be A Boy Worker
On
This Farm
I Carry My Basket
Under My Arm
And Pretend To Be
The Grown
Owner Of The Entire Territory
To The Far Hills Beyond

We Pretend A Farmer Planted This Tree
A Hundred Years Ago To Keep
The Strong West Winds From
Hitting
His House So Hard
Or Maybe
Those
Winds Carried Some Tree S e e d s
Over The Hill To Our Yard
We Will
Never Know But Those Black
Walnuts Make The Best Cake

Sunday Afternoon   Under A Warm Blue Sky

We Stop Our Game   To Notice A Busy Chip
                                            munk
Digging New Tunnels   At The Edge
                              Of Our Yard

Our Family Squirrel   Stops
                          In   Front   Of   His
                                    T r e e
With A Fresh Black Walnut   In His Mouth
We
See Him Go Up And Down That Tree   A l l
                              A f t e r n o o n
With Supplies For Long
                    Cold   M o n t h s

As A Cloud
Passes Over The Warm Sun   We Feel   That
                                        First
                                        Cool
                                        Hint

Aaron

My Older Brother
Once Told Me He
Was The Ruler Of   This Hedge
Last
Year I Had To Have Permission
To Pick Wild Violets   For Mom

This   Morning   Aaron
                                                    Sits
                                                    In A
                                                    School
And I Am   The New Boss
Of Hedge Trees
And Mole Holes
And Violets   And   Black Bugs
                                        Under
                                        Green
                                        Moss

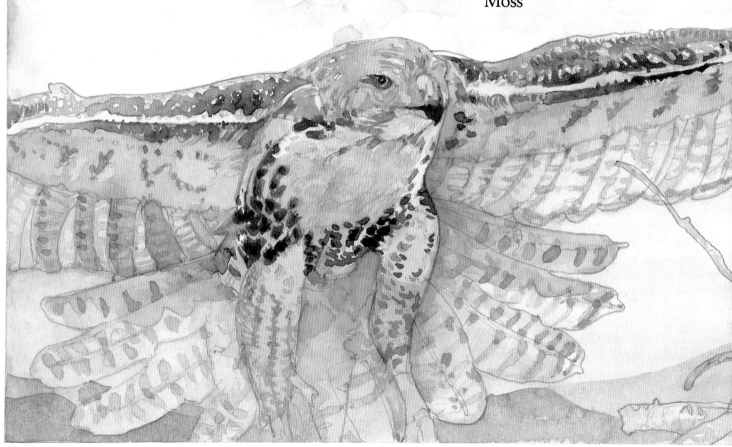

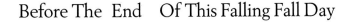

Before The End   Of This Falling Fall Day

When Night
        Means
                End Of Play
                And
                Put The Toys
                        A w a y
There Is Almost
            Dark   When The Field Is Full
                   Of S e c r e t s Under
                   The   H e a v y Hedge

Cicadas   Sound   Electric
Catbirds Sound Like Cats
Even Jays Are Fooled In
                        to
W a r n i n g   S q u a w k s

                            Hawks
                        C i r c l e
                            Their
                        Baby Hawks
                            Home

Granny's Ninety-Two-Year-Old Legs

Are Aching This October Morning   The Sun Is Bright   In The Pale
Blue
Sky
But She Says Her Shin Bones Have Been Hurting   Clear To   Winter

There Will Be   Falling
Weather   By The Feel Of Her Legs   And   She Knows
That   Barometer   At The Weather Station
Will   Follow   Right   Along   By   Evening
And There Will Be Cold And Rain Through
The Night

Granny's Ninety-Two-Year-Old Legs
Are
Almost
Always
Right

October
Afternoons   We Walk Around The House

Pulling Chair Cushions Into The   Garage
And Covering The Round White Table Where
We Ate Last S u m m e r ' s Snacks
And Stacking   All   The Chairs   And Tables
U n t i l N e x t S p r i n g
I   Bring
   Daddy
   Some
      Nails While He Hammers Bent Boards In
                                    to
      T h e O l d Y a r d F e n c e

Saturday   After Aaron's Soccer Game   He
                                        Gets
                                         To
      Walk The Dog Around Our   House
      While We Put   New Straw   Into
                                  The
                                  Dog
                                 House
      And A Nice Piece Of Purple Rug
      F o r T h e C o l d F l o o r

It Is Late

When We Walk   Back From Our Healthy Walk Tonight
The
Moon Is So Full   It Is Almost   Bursting   O   p   e   n
                   Like That Over
                        ripe   Pumpkin   In   Our
                                                G a r d e n

The
Moon Is Hanging Like That   Pumpkin
                                  Without   A   F a c e
                                                     Over
                                                      Our
                                               H e d g e

We Want To   Carve   A Face
Into
This Harvest Moon Tonight   And Have It   Grin   An
                            Autumn   Greeting
                            In The   Fall Air

                            Seeds Of   Starlight
                            S c a t t e r   Everywhere

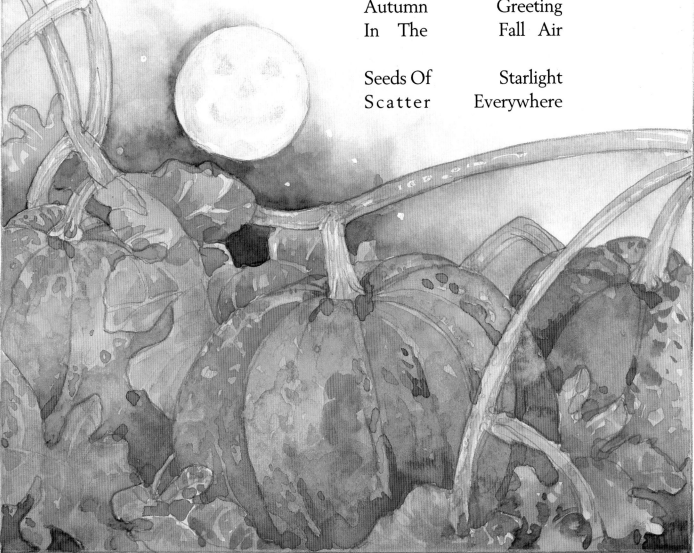

On   Limestone   Street

Where The   Open Field Is Longest   Back   To
The   Minnow   Stream   WePutOurBikesDown
                                            And L i s t e n
This Must Be The N o i s i e s t Day   Of   This
                                                   End   Of   This
                                                   Fall S e a s o n

Woodpeckers   Peck Wood
And Bluejays   Screech
And Each   Cold B r e e z e
                  Hard
Blows Branches   Shakes
                                      Leaves
Over Our Freezing Ears

Near Our Fence
Farmer Frances Is Cutting Dead Trees For Her
                                            W a r m i n g
                                                   F i r e s

We Will All Be
In   For Winter
Very   Soon